NORTH CAROLINA
The Tar Heel State

★

TEN TOP FACTS ABOUT NORTH CAROLIN

★ ★ ★ ★ ★ ★ ★ ★ ★ ★ ★ ★

•State nickname:	Tar Heel State, Old North State
•State motto:	*Esse Quam Videri* (To Be, Rather Than to Seem)
•Capital:	Raleigh
•Area:	48,718 square miles
•State flower:	Flowering dogwood
•State tree:	Longleaf pine
•State bird:	Cardinal
•State insect:	Honeybee
•State dog:	Plott hound
•State reptile:	Eastern box turtle

To my wife, Debra, and son, Zach, who shared North Carolina with me

p. 4: U.S. Mint; p. 5: (all) North Wind Picture Archives, Alfred, ME; p. 6: North Wind Picture Archives; p. 7: Courtesy of North Carolina Division of Archives and History, Raleigh, NC; p. 8: (top left) North Wind Picture Archives, (bottom left) Superstock Images, Jacksonville, FL, (top right) Brown Brothers, Sterling, PA; p. 9: (both) North Wind Picture Archives; p. 10: (both) Courtesy of North Carolina Divison of Archives and History; p. 11: (top left) Brown Brothers; p. 12: Superstock Images; p. 13: Brown Brothers; p. 14 (top) Corbis, New York, NY, (bottom right) Brown Brothers; p. 15: Superstock Images; p. 16: (both, top left) Brown Brothers, (top right) Corbis, (bottom right) Bernard Hoffman/TimePix, New York, NY; p. 17: Bettmann/Corbis; p. 18: (top left) North Carolina Travel & Tourism, Raleigh, NC, (top right) Superstock Images, (bottom right) William Ross/North Carolina Travel & Tourism; p. 19: Kelly Culpepper/Transparencies, Inc., Charlotte, NC; p. 20: (top left) North Carolina Travel & Tourism, (bottom left) Neil Rabinowitz/Corbis, (top right) North Carolina Travel & Tourism, (bottom right) Superstock Images; p. 21: (left) North Carolina Travel & Tourism, (top right) N. Carter/North Wind Picture Archives, (center right) Superstock Images; p. 22 (right top and center) North Carolina Travel & Tourism, North Carolina Division of Archives and History (Bradham), M. Barcellona/TimePix (Delany sisters); p. 23: Reuters NewMedia Inc./Corbis (Dole), Superstock Images (Graham), Henry Diltz/Corbis (Griffith), North Wind Picture Archives (Johnson); Steve Kagen/TimePix (Jordan), North Wind Picture Archives (Madison), George Tiedemann/TimePix, Brown Brothers (Wolfe); p. 25: North Wind Picture Archives.

Photo research by Dwayne Howard
All other illustrations by John Speirs

ISBN 0-439-22411-X

THE
Jim Henson
—COMPANY—

12 11 10 9 8 7 6 5 4 3 2 1   1 2 3 4 5 6

Designed by Madalina Stefan

Printed in the U.S.A.

First Scholastic printing, August 2001

Scholastic has a wide range of fun, high-quality book clubs for children of all ages. Please visit our Web site at www.scholastic.com/athomeclubs.

NORTH CAROLINA
The Tar Heel State

By Sean Stewart Price

SCHOLASTIC INC.

New York Toronto London Auckland Sydney Mexico City New Delhi Hong Kong Buenos Aires

A Celebration of the Fifty States

★ ★ ★ ★ ★ ★ ★ ★ ★ ★ ★ ★ ★

In January 1999, the U.S. Mint started an ambitious ten-year program to commemorate each of the fifty United States. Over the next several years (through 2008), they will issue five newly designed quarters each year.

One side (obverse) of each new quarter will display the profile of George Washington and the words *Liberty, In God We Trust,* and *United States of America.* The other side (reverse) will feature a design honoring a specific state's unique history, the year it became a state, the year of the quarter's issue, and the words *E Pluribus Unum* (Latin for "From many, one"). The quarters are being issued in the order in which the states joined the Union, beginning with the thirteen original colonies.

To find out more about the 50 State Quarters™ Program, visit the official U.S. Mint Web site at *www.USMINT.gov.*

NORTH CAROLINA'S QUARTER: First Flight

Before 1900, neither Orville nor Wilbur Wright had ever laid eyes on North Carolina. However, the two bicycle-makers from Dayton, Ohio, were determined to solve the mystery of flight, and they needed a testing ground for their gliders and airplanes. The place they had in mind had to be isolated, with strong winds and plenty of room for takeoffs. It also needed lots of sand to cushion landings. After a long search, the Wrights settled on the Kill Devil Hills area near Kitty Hawk, North Carolina.

Kitty Hawk is part of the Outer Banks, a chain of narrow, sandy islands along North Carolina's Atlantic coast. In the early 1900s, Kitty Hawk was an almost uninhabited, windswept island. The Wright brothers had to endure harsh weather and isolation while they learned to fly. Years of hard work finally paid off on the chilly morning of December 17, 1903, when they became the first people ever to fly a heavier-than-air craft. They soon earned worldwide reputations for their brilliance and daring. North Carolina's quarter commemorates the Wright brothers' achievements with an artist's rendition of their famous airplane and the inscription "First Flight."

Hernando de Soto

Sir Walter Raleigh

The New World

When Europeans first arrived in the area we now call North Carolina in the 1500s, they found an abundance of animals to hunt, good soil for growing crops, and friendly Native American tribes. At the time, an estimated 35,000 Indians from thirty different tribes lived on the land. Among the biggest tribes were the Tuscarora near the coast and in the central foothills (or Piedmont), the Hatteras along the coast, and the Cherokee in the western mountains.

In 1524, Italian explorer Giovanni da Verrazano, sailing for France, became the first European to explore North Carolina's coast. He stopped briefly on the Outer Banks — the sandy islands just off the mainland. Sixteen years later, Spanish explorer Hernando de Soto and 700 men trudged through the mountains of western North Carolina looking for gold. Had they traveled slightly farther to the east (near present-day Charlotte), they might have found it. Instead, de Soto and his men pressed westward and discovered the Mississippi River.

Sir Walter Raleigh, an English nobleman and explorer, established the first English colony in North America on Roanoke Island in 1585. He wanted to set up a military base there and to exploit the riches of the New World. Unfortunately, the 108 colonists (all men) fought with local Indians and wasted time looking for gold when they should have been hunting food. They soon returned to England.

In 1587, Raleigh sent a second group of colonists made up of ninety-one men, seventeen women, and nine children. However, the ships that were supposed to bring supplies to the colony were

Map of Raleigh's colony

Colonists landing on Roanoke Island

held up for three years by a war with Spain. When the ships finally arrived in 1590, Roanoke's colonists had disappeared. Nobody is sure what happened to the "Lost Colony of Roanoke." Some Indians later said that the colonists died in a battle between warring tribes. Others said that a few survivors married friendly Indians. Before they vanished, though, one couple gave birth to a baby girl named Virginia Dare. Like the others, her fate is unknown, but she is recognized as the first English child born in America.

Land of Charles

In 1629, British King Charles I tried to settle a large piece of land in the New World, later called *Carolana*, Latin for "Land of Charles." That tract of land included what is now North Carolina and South Carolina. The spelling was later changed to Carolina and the colony was divided into two colonies — North and South — in 1712.

Settlement of North Carolina did not begin in earnest until the 1660s. In 1663, British King Charles II granted control of North Carolina to eight noblemen called "lords proprietors." Unlike neighboring Virginia and South Carolina, North Carolina did not have a large port for ships. The currents and winds on its coast made sailing treacherous. Also, the western region of the colony was covered with mountains, and there were few good north-south roads. As a result, North Carolina became isolated from the rest of the world. Immigrants had a difficult time moving there, and the people who lived there often had no way to get their crops to market. This geographic isolation slowed North Carolina's growth for several centuries.

Likewise, the lords proprietors in England found it difficult to rule North Carolina from across the ocean. They angered many colonists by appointing governors who were corrupt. Also, Native American tribes became hostile toward the growing number of colonists on their land, and the proprietors seemed unable to defend against their attacks. Between 1664 and 1689, North Carolinians overthrew five of the governors appointed by the lords proprietors, choosing to run the colony themselves. Finally, in 1689, the proprietors found honest local men to govern the colony, and tensions eased.

As the political situation improved, a growing number of immigrants from Pennsylvania, South Carolina, and Virginia moved to North Carolina. They were looking for cheap land and greater freedom. By 1705, Bath — North Carolina's first town — had been incorporated. However, all immigrants and African slaves who came to North Carolina faced a period of illness that locals called "sea-soning." The mixture of diseases from three continents — Europe, Africa, and North America — killed off thousands of people. Children suffered the most among Europeans and slaves, but the situation was worse for Native Americans. Plagues from Europe, like smallpox, proved to be the deadliest. Indians died by the tens of thousands. It became harder and harder for them to defend their lands against the growing tide of European colonists.

Indians and Pirates

The Tuscarora Indians, the largest of the coastal tribes, hated the white colonists because they brought disease, kidnapped Indians as slaves, and monopolized their hunting grounds. On September 22, 1711, they launched a bloody assault on settlements throughout North Carolina. Hundreds of people were massacred before an army from South Carolina marched north to defeat the Tuscarora. The fighting finally ended in

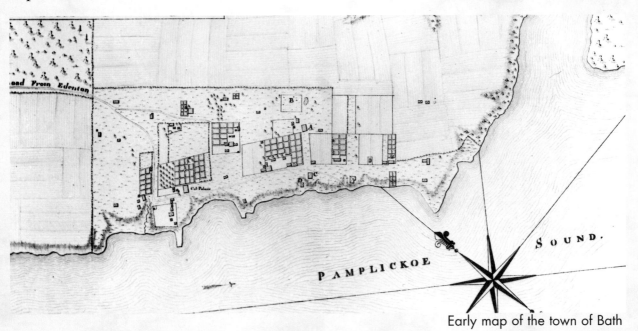

Early map of the town of Bath

Colonists fleeing during the Tuscarora War

Tobacco plantation

March 1713. The colony was devastated, but Indian attacks never again threatened its existence.

Around the same time, North Carolina's coastline was taken over by pirates. It was the perfect hiding place for fleeing criminals, with plenty of shallow creeks and coves where ships could hide. In 1718, expeditions from Virginia and South Carolina captured or killed several notorious pirates, including Blackbeard, the most feared outlaw.

The capture of Blackbeard

Tobacco and Tar

Since North Carolina's first days as a colony, tobacco has been one of its most important crops. Indians introduced the practice of smoking tobacco to the Spanish, and they in turn launched a smoking craze in Europe. During the 1700s, demand for tobacco on both sides of the Atlantic made the crop profitable.

The colony's first major industry was the production of wood, tar, and turpentine, all made from the huge pine forests in the east. These three products were called "naval stores" because of their usefulness in building ships. No one knows exactly where the state's nickname, the Tar Heel State, comes from, but many historians believe it dates from colonial times when the state was a leading producer of these products.

Carolina colonial family

A Royal Colony

In 1729, King George III bought North Carolina back from the lords proprietors. It became a royal colony ruled directly by the king. This gave North Carolinians more control over their own affairs. Between 1730 and 1775, the colony's population soared from about 36,000 to nearly 350,000. The area between the coast and the mountains — called the Piedmont — filled rapidly with small farmers. Piedmont towns like Fayetteville, Charlotte, and Salem (later Winston-Salem) also sprang up.

In the years just before the American Revolution, North Carolina's white population was sharply divided. Most of the wealthy people in the state lived near the coast, and a handful of plantation owners controlled the colonial government. By 1770, more than half of North Carolina's people were small farmers living in the western counties. Some westerners formed an armed band, called the Regulators, and demanded more control of the government. In 1771, the Regulators lost the Battle of Alamance Creek to royal militia near Chapel Hill, and their movement fizzled. Several colonists, however, continued to hope for independence from England and the king.

The royal militia defeating the Regulators

Cape Fear patriots resisting the British fleet

The American Revolution

During the French and Indian War (1754–1763), Great Britain battled France and its Indian allies for control of North America. The British finally won, but at great cost. In the 1760s, they passed a series of taxes and restrictive trade laws to pay for the war. The Stamp Act of 1765, for instance, taxed all paper items from legal documents to newspapers. The heavy tax burden it imposed caused fierce protests in the port city of Wilmington. The Stamp Act was repealed but was soon replaced by other harsh laws like the Townshend Acts of 1767 (which taxed paper, glass, and other items) and the Quartering Act of 1774 (which allowed British soldiers to take over private homes). These laws greatly angered American colonists.

The colonists' unrest led to the start of the American Revolution on April 19, 1775, with the battles of Lexington and Concord in Massachusetts. North Carolina was the first colony to instruct its delegates at the Continental Congress in Philadelphia to vote for independence. In July 1776, North Carolinians Joseph Hewes, William Hooper, and John Penn signed the Declaration of Independence. Just a few months before, in February 1776, patriots and loyalists had squared off at the Battle of Moore's Creek Bridge near Wilmington. The crushing patriot victory there kept North Carolina from falling into British hands.

Reenactment of Battle of Moore's Creek Bridge

The Battle of Guilford Courthouse

Thousands of men from North Carolina joined the Continental army, yet few battles were actually fought in the state. The biggest was the Battle of Guilford Courthouse on March 15, 1781, in which about 300 Americans and 530 British died. The British were so badly weakened that they had to leave the Carolinas. Seven months later, George Washington defeated the British at Yorktown, Virginia, effectively ending the war.

In 1787, the thirteen states that made up the United States of America wrote a new constitution in Philadelphia. Though North Carolina's own Dr. Hugh Williamson helped to write the document, opposition to it in his home state was fierce. Many North Carolinians feared that a strong federal government would take away the rights they had won during the Revolution. The state rejected the document at first, but once the Bill of Rights was added in 1789, North Carolina became the twelfth state to ratify the Constitution.

Gold!

In 1799, twelve-year-old Conrad Reed discovered a large glittering rock while fishing near his home in Carrabus County. Reed liked it so much that he took the seventeen-pound rock home, where his father used it as a doorstop. Mr. Reed finally took it to a jeweler in 1802, and it turned out to be gold. So began the first gold rush in U.S. history. Later, prospectors found nuggets as large as twenty-eight pounds, and for several decades North Carolina and Georgia remained the top gold-producing states in the country. By the 1850s, though, North Carolina's gold had mostly all been mined and richer deposits lured prospectors to California.

While the gold rush helped North Carolina to flourish in the early 1800s, little was done to help the state's geographic isolation. State lawmakers failed to build roads or develop trade. Although the first state university in the country, the University of North Carolina, was created in 1795, the state's educational system saw little improvement. As a result, most North Carolinians remained uneducated and cut off from the world. Outsiders who visited sleepy North Carolina called it the "Rip Van Winkle State." Rip Van Winkle was a character from a Washington Irving story who slept for twenty years and awoke to find everything around him changed.

This slow progress caused more than 400,000 North Carolinians to seek their fortunes elsewhere in the late 1700s and early 1800s. By 1850, at least thirty-one percent of all native North Carolinians lived in another state. Among those who headed west were future Presidents Andrew Jackson, Andrew Johnson, and James K. Polk.

A Time of Change

As settlers moved west, they snatched up the mountainous lands of North Carolina, Tennessee, and Georgia that belonged to the Cherokee. While in office in 1830, President Andrew Jackson had backed the Indian Removal Act that led to the forced removal of the Cherokee in 1838. Cherokee men, women, and children had to walk more than 1,000 miles to present-day Oklahoma, and nearly one-fourth died along the way. About 1,000 Cherokee stayed behind, hiding in the mountains of North Carolina. Some of their descendants still live in the state today on the Cherokee Indian Reservation.

Cherokees go west

Carting tobacco to the warehouse

Over the next several years, more and more slaves were brought from Africa to work on the many cotton and tobacco plantations in the eastern coastal region of the state. Life was brutally tough for North Carolina slaves, as one of them recalled: "They drove us from sunup till sunset. . . . We hated to see the sun rise in slavery time, because it meant another hard day." During the 1830s, the state legislature made life even harder for African-Americans, passing laws that restricted their movement and denied free blacks the right to vote. Even so, large pockets of white antislavery advocates existed in the Piedmont and western mountains.

Around this time, many North Carolinians grew tired of their state's reputation for backwardness. In 1835, overdue political reforms gave people in the western part of the state fair representation in the legislature. New roads and schools were built, and dozens of new newspapers helped inform people throughout the state. Railroad workers laid more than 900 miles of railroad track before 1860, which helped both farmers and the state's budding textile industry. On the eve of the Civil War, North Carolina still had a long way to go economically to catch up with the rest of the country, but it could no longer be called the "Rip Van Winkle State."

Battle of Bentonville

The Civil War

At the outbreak of the Civil War in 1861, North Carolina was once again divided geographically and politically. In the east, where slavery was a way of life, people strongly favored joining the Confederacy. In the west, where slavery was rare, most people backed the Union. North Carolina became the last state to join the Confederacy. Many North Carolinians felt duty bound to defend their fellow Southerners. North Carolina furnished about one-sixth of all the South's troops, and it lost more men in combat — about 40,000 — than any other Southern state.

As the war dragged on, strong sentiment to rejoin the Union swelled in North Carolina, and the state came close to leaving the Confederacy. Wartime experiences in North Carolina differed by region. In coastal cities like Wilmington, the focus was on getting supply ships through the Union naval blockade. In the western mountains, small bands of pro-Union and pro-Confederate sympathizers ambushed each other. In March 1865, Union General William T. Sherman defeated a smaller Confederate army led by Joseph E. Johnston at the Battle of Bentonville in the Piedmont — the site of the last major battle of the war.

General Joseph E. Johnston

A Shattered State

During the period known as Reconstruction, former slaves joined the Republican Party because it was the party of Abraham Lincoln. Republicans — both black and white — controlled North Carolina's state government for about five years. But white terrorist groups like the Ku Klux Klan formed and used violence to scare away black voters. Republican support dropped, and by 1870, the whites-only Democratic Party seized control of state offices. By 1900, North Carolina lawmakers had passed harsh "Jim Crow" laws that robbed blacks of basic rights, like voting, and enforced racial segregation.

The war and its aftermath left North Carolina desperately poor. Most people still farmed the land, raising cotton, tobacco, and corn. However, by 1900, North Carolina's cheap pool of labor spurred the creation of 7,266 factories — most of them textile mills — that employed more than 70,000 people. Working in the mill was safer and more stable than farming. But millworkers still labored twelve hours each day for little more than a penny's wage.

New Beginnings

With the dawn of the twentieth century, North Carolina finally rose out of its long isolation. North Carolina's soaring mountains had attracted tourists since colonial days. But when doctors in the early 1900s began recommending mountain air as

Workers in a textile mill, 1900

15

James Duke

Benjamin Duke

Building roads

being particularly healthy, rich tourists came to western North Carolina in droves and became enchanted with its natural beauty. Industry thrived as well. The brothers James and Benjamin Duke of Durham controlled ninety percent of America's cigarette production. North Carolina's abundant supply of wood and cheap labor also made it a center for furniture making. By the early 1900s, furniture, textiles, and tobacco were the state's "Big Three" industries.

North Carolina soon became known as the most progressive state in the South. Governor Charles B. Aycock overhauled the state's education system from 1901 to 1905, building 1,200 new schools and raising teachers' salaries. In the 1920s, the Duke brothers took over a small Methodist college in Durham and turned it into Duke University, one of the finest schools in the country. Around the same time, people started calling North Carolina the "Good Roads State" after the government built more than 6,000 miles of new roads. Unfortunately, the Great Depression, which began in 1929, curtailed many of these improvements. Factories closed and farmers were wiped out. Thousands found themselves jobless and penniless.

It took World War II (1939–1945) to pull North Carolina completely out of the Depression. The state was home to several military bases, including Fort Bragg at Fayetteville, one of the country's largest. North Carolina textile factories produced socks, blankets, parachutes, and other supplies for soldiers.

Communications post at Fort Bragg, 1942

16

Winning Civil Rights

After World War II, as in most of the South, North Carolina remained segregated. Blacks were not allowed to enter the same restaurants, stores, or theaters as whites. They were also forced to attend separate, poorly funded schools. In 1954, the U.S. Supreme Court ruled that having separate schools for blacks and whites was unconstitutional. Yet white North Carolinians refused to integrate schools and other facilities.

On February 1, 1960, four black college students from Greensboro decided to act against the segregation. Ezell Blair Jr., Franklin McCain, Joseph McNeil, and David Richmond sat down at the local Woolworth's lunch counter and refused to leave until they were served. Their protest inspired other "sit-ins" throughout the rest of the South, and this tactic became a favorite course of action during the civil rights movement. The Greensboro sit-in worked: Woolworth's and other stores in the area agreed to serve black patrons.

However, it took federal civil rights laws, passed in 1964 and 1965, to end segregation forever in North Carolina. Even then, racial problems continued to flare. During the early 1970s, both Wilmington and Charlotte endured bitter racial unrest over the issue of school integration. And in 1979, Ku Klux Klansmen and neo-Nazis killed five protesters at an anti-Klan rally. Despite these and other problems, more than 100,000 African-Americans who had once fled to the North began returning home during the 1970s.

Sit-in at Woolworth's lunch counter

North Carolina Today

Nantahala Gorge in the Great Smoky Mountains

Tobacco harvest

In some important ways, North Carolina has changed little in the last 100 years. The same "Big Three" industries — furniture, textiles, and tobacco — remain vital to the state's economy. But the state has become more diverse. Charlotte is now the second most important banking center in the United States, trailing only New York. The Raleigh-Durham-Chapel Hill area is now a leader in industries such as biotechnology and computers, thanks to the Research Triangle Park. The park allows companies like IBM and Verizon to tap the brainpower of three nearby universities — North Carolina State University at Raleigh, the University of North Carolina at Chapel Hill, and Duke University of Durham. Traditionally an agricultural state, only one percent of North Carolina's economic growth comes from farm products like tobacco, hogs, and corn.

Tourism, on the other hand, has become a major industry in North Carolina. More than forty-four million people descend upon the state each year to hike in the Great Smoky Mountains or sunbathe on the beaches of the Outer Banks. The state's warm climate year-round makes it an attractive place to live. Far from being a sleepy backwater, North Carolina has become a leader among states.

Outer Banks

View from Blue Ridge Parkway in the fall

Things to Do and Places to See

Battleship U.S.S. North Carolina

During World War II, the battleship *U.S.S. North Carolina* took part in every major Pacific offensive. Almost scrapped by the U.S. Navy in the 1950s, the ship was taken to Wilmington and turned into a memorial in 1961. Today, visitors can inspect the old battleship and visit its museum.

Biltmore Estate

The United States may not have royalty, but it does have castles. The Biltmore Estate outside of Asheville is the largest private residence in the country. Constructed in the 1890s for a member of the wealthy Vanderbilt family, it features breathtaking art and architecture and impressive gardens.

Blue Ridge Parkway

The Blue Ridge Parkway winds through mountainous western North Carolina, making it one of the most scenic drives in the United States. Just off the parkway are countless attractions, including ski resorts, hiking trails, campgrounds, the Tweetsie Railroad theme park, and a beautiful view of Mount Mitchell, the highest peak in North America east of the Mississippi River (6,684 feet).

Great Smoky Mountains National Park

The Blue Ridge Parkway begins (or ends, depending on which way you're going) at the Great Smoky Mountains National Park. Straddling the border of North Carolina and

Tennessee, it is the most-visited national park in the country. Within its 520,408 acres are 1,500 species of flowering plants, 200 species of birds, and 60 species of mammals. The most popular mammals are the black bears, which frequently can be seen fishing and romping around.

Preparing to race

Lowe's Motor Speedway

Stock car racing is practically a religion in North Carolina, and one of its cathedrals is Lowe's Motor Speedway just north of Charlotte. Every May, more than 187,000 spectators flock there to watch the Coca-Cola 600, NASCAR's longest race.

Farmstead interior, Oconaluftee Indian Village

Oconaluftee Indian Village

The Oconaluftee Indian Village is a re-creation of a 1750 Cherokee village that lies just outside the Cherokee Indian Reservation in western

North Carolina. From May through October, you can see how Cherokees once built homes, made dugout canoes, and prepared food. Nearby is the Museum of the Cherokee Indian, which is open year-round. During the summer, you can see *Unto These Hills,* an outdoor drama documenting Cherokee history.

Cape Hatteras Lighthouse

Outer Banks

Beautiful beaches and rich history make the Outer Banks, the strip of sandy islands just off North Carolina's coastline, one of the state's most popular tourist destinations. The most famous of North Carolina's eight lighthouses is on the Outer Banks at Cape Hatteras. It still warns ships about a dangerous patch of ocean called "the Graveyard of the Atlantic," where fickle winds and currents have caused more than 5,000 shipwrecks.

North Carolina Zoological Park

The North Carolina Zoological Park near Asheboro is the country's largest walk-through natural habitat zoo. Nearly five miles of trails

Ape at the North Carolina Zoo

snake through 500 acres of exhibits. The zoo's more than 1,000 animals include polar bears, sea lions, bison, giraffes, and other wildlife from North America and Africa.

Roller coaster at Carowinds

Paramount's Carowinds

Just south of Charlotte is Paramount's Carowinds, a 100-acre water and theme park on the North Carolina/South Carolina border. State-of-the-art roller coasters, 3-D movie simulators, a four-story rafting ride, and huge tube slides draw many visitors.

Famous People from North Carolina

Caleb Bradham (1867–1934)

Most people don't know who Caleb Bradham is, but they know the product he invented. In 1896, Bradham, a pharmacist in New Bern, North Carolina, wanted to create a drink that would help cure stomach upset and taste good, too. The formula he came up with was for Pepsi-Cola. By 1902, his new drink was so popular that he founded the company known today as Pepsico.

Bessie Delany (1891–1995)
Sadie Delany (1889–1999)

In 1991, the *New York Times* published an article about Bessie and Sadie Delany, two elderly black sisters who were both more than 100 years old. The Delanys were born and raised in Raleigh and clearly remembered the daily insults they suffered because of their skin color. Neither sister ever married, but both moved to New York City and became successful career women. They also rubbed shoulders with important black artists like poet Langston Hughes and actor Paul Robeson. The article led to a best-selling book called *Having Our Say: The Delany Sisters' First 100 Years* and was followed by a popular play based on their lives.

Elizabeth Dole (1936–)

A Salisbury native, Elizabeth Dole is one of the leading female politicians in the United States. During the 1980s, she served as both Secretary of Transportation and Secretary of Labor. During the 1990s, she was president of the American Red Cross. She helped her husband, Republican Senator Robert Dole, in his unsuccessful 1996 bid to become President. Elizabeth Dole then ran for President in the 2000 election but was unable to obtain the Republican nomination.

Billy Graham (1918–)

Few religious leaders have had the influence of Charlotte native Billy Graham. In the 1940s, he was an energetic Protestant evangelist who caught the eye of the national news media and he was catapulted to worldwide fame. Graham has evangelized to stadium-sized crowds around the world, and he has been a religious adviser to every U.S. President since the 1950s.

Andy Griffith (1926–)

Andy Griffith is one of the most beloved television actors of all time. He is most famous for *The Andy Griffith Show,* which showed an idealized version of small-town life. Griffith based the fictional town of Mayberry on his real hometown of Mount Airy. The show won high ratings at the time and has remained popular in syndication.

Andrew Johnson (1808–1875)

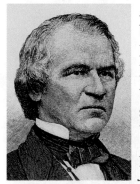

Andrew Johnson was born and raised in Raleigh. As a teenager, he left for Tennessee, where he became a successful tailor and U.S. senator. President Abraham Lincoln made Johnson his vice president, and Johnson rose to the presidency when Lincoln was shot in 1865. Johnson disagreed strongly with Congress over postwar policies and became the first President ever to be impeached. He avoided being removed from office by a narrow margin of one vote.

Michael Jordan (1963–)

North Carolina's universities have always competed fiercely on the basketball court, making the state a hoop fan's paradise. So it is fitting that the greatest basketball player in history, Michael Jordan, was raised in Wilmington. In 1982, Jordan helped lead the University of North Carolina to the NCAA championship while still a freshman. In the NBA, he led the Chicago Bulls to four world championships. Though retired, Jordan remains the most recognized athlete in the world.

Dolley Madison (1768–1849)

Dolley Madison, wife of President James Madison, was one of the most remarkable first ladies in U.S. history. During the War of 1812, when British soldiers burned Washington, D.C., Madison saved important state papers and a famous painting of George Washington from the flames. Born and raised in Guilford County, North Carolina, Madison was known for being a witty and strong-minded woman.

Richard Petty (1937–)

Richard Petty's career as a stock car racer began in 1958 and ended in 1992. During that time, he won more than 200 races and made more money than any stock car driver in history. Between 1964 and 1981, he won the Daytona 500 and the NASCAR national championship each seven times. Born in Level Cross, North Carolina, Petty is affectionately known as "King Richard."

Thomas Wolfe (1900–1938)

Thomas Wolfe was born and raised in Asheville, and he became famous for writing novels based on his own life. He was one of America's top authors in the 1930s. Wolfe's poetic descriptions of life in the North Carolina mountains still have great power. Among his most famous novels are *Look Homeward, Angel* (1929) and *You Can't Go Home Again* (1940).

O. Henry's Gift

O. Henry (1862–1910) was the pen name of Greensboro native William Sydney Porter. In the early 1900s, Porter became the best-known short-story writer in the United States. At age twenty, he left North Carolina and moved to Texas, working first as a bank teller and then as a journalist. In 1898, he was convicted of stealing money from the bank where he had worked.

When Porter emerged from prison three years later, he began writing short stories for newspapers and magazines. He soon moved to New York and became famous for stories that romanticized commonplace people and things. His stories also delivered a surprise twist at the end that kept the reader guessing. This is a shortened version of one of O. Henry's most famous stories, "The Gift of the Magi."

One dollar and eighty-seven cents. That was all. Three times Della counted it. Tomorrow would be Christmas Day, and she had only $1.87 with which to buy Jim a present. She had been saving every penny she could for months, with this result.

Now, there were two possessions of the James Dillingham Youngs in which they both took a mighty pride. One was Jim's gold watch that had been his father's and his grandfather's. The other was Della's hair.

So now Della's beautiful hair fell about her rippling and shining like a cascade of brown waters. It reached below her knee and made itself almost a garment for her.

On went her old brown jacket; on went her old brown hat. With a whirl of skirts and with the brilliant sparkle still in her eyes, she fluttered out the door and down the stairs to the street.

Where she stopped the sign read: "Mme. Sofronie. Hair Goods of All Kinds." One flight up Della ran, and collected herself, panting. Madame, large, too white, chilly, hardly looked the "Sofronie."

"Will you buy my hair?" asked Della.

"I buy hair," said Madame. "Take yer hat off and let's have a sight at the looks of it."

Down rippled the brown cascade.

"Twenty dollars," said Madame, lifting the mass with a practiced hand.

"Give it to me quick," said Della.

Oh, and the next two hours tripped by on rosy wings. She was ransacking the stores for Jim's present.

She found it at last. It surely had been made for Jim and no one else. It was a platinum fob chain simple and chaste in design. . . . It was even worthy of The Watch.

At 7 o'clock the coffee was made and the frying-pan was on the back of the stove hot and ready to cook the chops.

Della doubled the fob chain in her hand and sat on the corner of the table near the door that he always entered.

The door opened and Jim stopped inside the door, as immovable as a setter at the scent of quail. His eyes were fixed upon Della, and there was an expression in them that she could not read, and it terrified her. It was not anger, nor surprise, nor disapproval, nor horror, nor any of the sentiments that she had been prepared for. He simply stared at her fixedly with that peculiar expression on his face.

"Jim, darling," she cried, "don't look at me that way. I had my hair cut off and sold because I couldn't have lived through Christmas without giving you a present. It'll grow out again — you won't mind, will you?"

"You've cut off your hair?" asked Jim, laboriously, as if he had not arrived at that patent fact yet even after the hardest mental labor.

"Cut it off and sold it," said Della. "Don't you like me just as well, anyhow? I'm me without my hair, ain't I?"

Jim looked about the room curiously.

"You say your hair is gone?" he said, with an air almost of idiocy.

"You needn't look for it," said Della. "It's sold, I tell you — sold and gone, too. It's Christmas Eve, boy. Be good to me, for it went for you. Maybe the hairs of my head were numbered," she went on with sudden serious sweetness, "but nobody could ever count my love for you. Shall I put the chops on, Jim?"

Jim drew a package from his overcoat pocket and threw it upon the table.

"Don't make any mistake, Dell," he said, "about me. I don't think there's anything in the way of a haircut or a shave or a shampoo that could make me like my girl any less. But if you'll unwrap that package you may see why you had me going a while at first."

White fingers and nimble tore at the string and paper. And then an ecstatic scream of joy; and then, alas! a quick feminine change to hysterical tears and wails, necessitating the immediate employment of all the comforting powers of the lord of the flat.

For there lay The Combs — the set of combs, side and back, that Della had worshiped long in a Broadway window. Beautiful combs, pure tortoise shell, with jewelled rims — just the shade to wear in the beautiful vanished hair. And now, they were hers, but the tresses that should have adorned the coveted adornments were gone.

But she hugged them to her bosom, and at length she was able to look up with dim eyes and a smile and say: "My hair grows so fast, Jim!"

And then Della leaped up like a little singed cat and cried, "Oh, oh!"

Jim had not yet seen his beautiful present. She held it out to him eagerly upon her open palm. The dull precious metal seemed to flash with a reflection of her bright and ardent spirit.

"Isn't it a dandy, Jim? I hunted all over town to find it. You'll have to look at the time a hundred times a day now. Give me your watch. I want to see how it looks on it."

Instead of obeying, Jim tumbled down on the couch and put his hands under the back of his head and smiled.

"Dell," said he, "let's put our Christmas presents away and keep 'em a while. They're too nice to use just at present. I sold the watch to get the money to buy your combs. And now suppose you put the chops on."

The magi, as you know, were wise men — wonderfully wise men — who brought gifts to the Babe in the manger. They invented the art of giving Christmas presents. Being wise, their gifts were no doubt wise ones, possibly bearing the privilege of exchange in case of duplication. And here I have lamely related to you the uneventful chronicle of two foolish children in a flat who most unwisely sacrificed for each other the greatest treasures of their house. But in a last word to the wise of these days, let it be said that of all who give gifts these two were the wisest. Of all who give and receive gifts, such as they are wisest. Everywhere they are wisest. They are the magi.

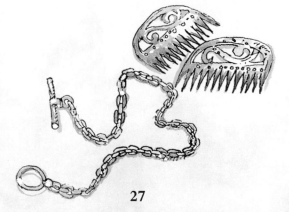

Carolina Barbecue

Pork has always been a favorite food in North Carolina, and hog farming is now the state's leading source of farm income. Not surprisingly, North Carolina has become famous for its barbecued pork. Be sure to have an adult supervise any chopping or cooking.

Barbecued Ribs

1 cup packed light brown sugar
1 tablespoon dry mustard
1 cup ketchup
Salt and pepper as needed
Pork ribs as needed

Mix the brown sugar, dry mustard, and ketchup in a large bowl. Also include small amounts of salt and pepper. You might want to add more after giving the sauce a taste test. Rinse the ribs in water, pat them dry, and then put them in the sauce. Cover the bowl and put it in the refrigerator for three to four hours. Remove the ribs and save the leftover sauce. Grill the ribs until they are done, basting frequently with the remaining sauce.